English

A review of inspection findings 1993/94

A report from the Office of Her Majesty's Chief Inspector of Schools

London: HMSO

Office for Standards in Education
Alexandra House
29–33 Kingsway
London WC2B 6SE

Telephone 0171-421 6800

Contents

Annex B 29–35

GCE AS and A-level results 1994 for English Language,
English Literature, Communication Studies and Drama

Introduction

This subject profile for English provides a review of the findings from inspections conducted for and by OFSTED during the academic year 1993/94. It continues the publication by OFSTED of reports on the quality of provision for and standards achieved in English. It includes information and discussion about aspects of inspecting English.

The secondary schools were inspected for OFSTED by teams led by Registered Inspectors. The teams which inspected primary schools were led by Her Majesty's Inspectors of Schools (HMI), and usually included independent inspectors in training.

Comments on secondary schools are based on evidence from some 600 inspections and those on primary from 112. The findings on primary schools need to be treated with caution because of the small size of the sample. There is insufficient evidence to comment on language and literacy in under-fives' education.

Data relating to middle schools are subsumed under Key Stage 2 or Key Stage 3 as appropriate.

Those sections of this profile concerned with inspection developments in English have drawn on additional evidence including that from the monitoring of inspections undertaken by HMI, the scrutiny of subject inspection evidence and English sections in inspection reports.

Subject Report

Main Findings

- Across all key stages, standards of achievement in English are satisfactory or better in four-fifths of schools. Standards are good or very good in almost 35%. Pupils are generally gaining understanding, knowledge and skills in all attainment targets though standards in writing are lower than those in reading, speaking and listening. (Paragraphs 1–13)

- Standards are higher at Key Stage 1, Key Stage 4 and post-16 than in the intermediate stages. At Key Stages 2 and 3 standards relating to at least one attainment target in English are unsatisfactory or poor in up to a quarter of schools. The equivalent proportions are approximately one-fifth for Key Stage 1, and one-seventh for Key Stage 4. (Paragraphs 1, 4, 9, 13)

- In the schools where standards are too low, deficiencies in the pupils' abilities to read, write, speak or listen inhibit their progress in all aspects of the curriculum, not just in English. (Paragraphs 1–13)

- The influence of the National Curriculum programmes of study is most marked at Key Stage 1. In a small minority of schools at Key Stages 2 and 3, insufficient attention is given to the programmes of study. Effective assessment by teachers is too often weak at these stages. At Key Stage 4, GCSE syllabuses are the main influence in the English curriculum and its assessment. Pupils' work does not always reflect the full range of study required by the National Curriculum at this stage. (Paragraphs 22–29)

- The quality of teaching is satisfactory or better in 80% of lessons across all stages. It is good or very good in almost 45% of them. There are some persistent weaknesses in teachers' knowledge and expertise : knowledge about formal aspects of language, particularly grammar and syntax; the development of reading at Key Stage 2 and Key Stage 3; the development of speaking and listening, particularly at Key Stage 2. Overall, pupils of high ability experience better teaching than those of average or low ability at all stages though this is not a significant feature of mixed ability classes in primary schools. (Paragraphs 14–20)

- Standards of achievement are influenced positively not only by the quality of the teaching but also by the quality with which the subject is managed in the school. There is scope for improvement of subject management at departmental level in middle and secondary schools and through subject co-ordinators in primary schools. (Paragraphs 27–31)

- A significant minority of schools lacks the book resources to develop fully the reading ability of all pupils. (Paragraphs 29–31)

- The relatively poor performance of boys in English is strongly evident from both examination results and ability setting even though they are often dominant in classroom discussion. (Paragraphs 15, 39)

Key issues for schools

Primary

Primary schools should:

- ensure that all aspects of the writing programmes of study are taught effectively to pupils in Key Stages 1 and 2.

- create regular and carefully planned opportunities for pupils to develop in speaking and listening, especially at Key Stage 2.

- attend particularly to the development of reading skills for all pupils at Key Stage 2 and to providing for them a wide and challenging range of reading material.

- seek to provide a suitably experienced language co-ordinator with the time and resources to influence positively the teaching of English throughout the school.

Secondary

Secondary schools should:

- ensure, by means of further training if necessary, that teachers of English at Key Stage 3 know how to improve the reading skills of all pupils, including the most able.

- provide regular and well-organised opportunities for all pupils to meet the National Curriculum attainment targets required for speaking and listening.

- take early and vigorous action to identify and remedy serious weaknesses in pupils' writing.

- encourage effective subject management through departmental, faculty or other suitable structures and require rapid improvement where management is weak.

All Schools

All schools should:

- ensure that all pupils develop technical and organisational skills in writing systematically.

- provide training where necessary to improve the teachers' subject knowledge about formal aspects of language, particularly grammar and syntax, and about suitable literature, particularly poetry.

- take all possible steps to bring about a rapid improvement in the performance of boys in English.

Standards of achievement

The GCSE and GCE results achieved nationally in English in 1994 are addressed in a section commencing at paragraph 47.

Key Stage 1

1   The standards of achievement relative to pupils' capabilities are satisfactory or better in the large majority of schools in this small sample. Standards are satisfactory or better in 82% of lessons at Key Stage 1. The percentage of lessons which are better than satisfactory is 28%. Standards in reading and in speaking and listening are better than those in writing. In up to a fifth of schools there is scope for considerable improvement in at least one of the aspects of the pupils' writing for which the National Curriculum provides an attainment target.

Speaking and Listening

2   In nearly all schools, children learn to listen attentively, to speak with confidence and to ask questions thoughtfully. Most can read simple texts aloud intelligently. Standards are high in about a quarter of schools, where pupils express themselves confidently in a wide range of circumstances, for example through role play and collaborative group work, with a good response evident to music and poetry. Low standards are apparent in a small minority of school where the pupils, particularly the less able, typically do not talk purposefully enough, ask questions or contribute to discussion from their own experience.

Reading

3   In most schools pupils acquire satisfactory phonic skills and a range of strategies for understanding printed texts. In over a third of

schools there are high expectations of all pupils with the result that, for example, second language learners reach competent standards by the end of the key stage and average as well as able pupils demonstrate a good standard of independent reading. In about 5% of schools standards are too low; pupils show little understanding of what they read, they have no systematic grasp of necessary skills and even able pupils do not become independent readers.

Writing

4   Typically, although standards in writing are at least satisfactory in nearly four-fifths of schools, there is too great an unevenness in the pupils' development of necessary skills, particularly handwriting and spelling. Good standards, which are found in about a fifth of schools, are marked by effective writing for different purposes, a developing sense of the usefulness of drafting and growing skills of sentence construction and vocabulary. Handwriting and spelling are developed systematically and there is some use of information technology (IT). Standards are too low in just over a fifth of schools where pupils do not progress quickly enough; for example, in developing their handwriting, the range of writing is too restricted and tasks are often undemanding for the more able.

Key Stage 2

5   Standards of achievement relative to pupils' capabilities are satisfactory or better in the majority of schools in this small sample. There is some evidence that pupils in the middle ability range do relatively better than the most or least able. The percentage of lessons where standards are satisfactory or better is 77%. The percentage of better than satisfactory is 21%. As in Key Stage 1, standards in writing are not as high as those in reading, speaking and listening. The proportion of schools where standards are too low in relation to at least one attainment target in English rises to nearly a quarter at this key stage.

Speaking and Listening

6   In most schools, pupils extend their speaking and listening skills successfully and develop their understanding of the purposes and importance of talk. In over a third of schools pupils build successfully

on Key Stage 1 and develop to a good standard their ability to structure an argument, express a point of view and listen to others' responses. In about one in ten, too many pupils cannot adequately present information, describe events or debate issues and systematic development of speaking and listening is too often neglected.

Reading

7   Reading standards are satisfactory or better in nine out of ten schools. Pupils achieve good standards of reading in about one-third of schools where they build on and develop systematically the skills they have learnt in Key Stage 1 in skimming, for example, or in deduction or in using texts for information. The variety of their reading increases, they talk about it in structured ways and use reading regularly for an increasing range of purposes such as information seeking and retrieval or as support for their work in drama. In about 10% of schools standards are too low. There is little expectation of progress; the pupils' experience of reading is too narrow, lacking in poetry especially, and they suffer from an absence of direct teaching of reading skills.

Writing

8   Good standards in writing are evident in only one in seven schools at this key stage, a proportion which is lower than those for other aspects of English. However, in about three-quarters of the schools, pupils achieve at least a competent standard. They are able to use redrafting skills to improve their work and know how to develop, for example, spelling by the use of dictionaries and other sources of support. Their handwriting is legible and well developed and many have begun to understand how to present their work for varying purposes and readers. In more than a fifth of schools, low standards result from too little attention being given to skills such as handwriting and spelling or to the range and extent of writing assignments. There is too much use of decontextualised and undemanding exercises which do little to improve the pupils' knowledge, understanding or skills.

Key Stages 3 and 4

9   Standards of achievement are somewhat higher at Key Stage 4 than at Key Stage 3. They are satisfactory or better in 84% of lessons in Key Stage 3, and better than satisfactory in 36%. The equivalent figures for Key Stage 4 are 86% and 39%. The evidence points to a positive correlation between standards on the one hand and the quality of teaching, learning and departmental management on the other. Standards also tend to be high when speaking and listening, reading and writing are interrelated. The relative weaknesses noted in the earlier key stages persist, especially in writing.

Speaking and Listening

10   The majority of pupils develop their speaking and listening abilities satisfactorily. Where standards are high pupils demonstrate that they can contribute effectively both in whole class discussions and in small groups. They speak with confidence, sustain concentration and argument and have learnt to listen with attention to others. These qualities are particularly evident at Key Stage 4 where over one-third of pupils attain high standards. At Key Stage 3, including the upper forms in middle schools, the majority of pupils perform positively in collaborative groups and drama activities which increase their confidence and provide a structure for speaking and listening. At both key stages, combinations of activities such as listening to tapes or stories and subsequently writing about them in some instances provide evidence of high standards of listening and response. Low standards are evident most frequently when opportunities for talk are limited or poorly organised, so that talk is unfocused and rambling, or pupils are not challenged to justify the opinions they express. Then, there is little sustained or critical exchange, teachers tend to dominate, and appropriate registers and forms of language are under-exploited. At Key Stage 3 standards are too low in one in six schools, slightly more than at Key Stage 4. Too often, boys dominate class discussions at the expense of girls.

Reading

11   Most pupils can read to an acceptable standard but there is too large a gap between the performances of the most and least able. Reading standards are too low in a fifth of schools at Key Stage 3 and in one in six schools at Key Stage 4. Strengths clearly outweigh weaknesses in about half the schools at both Key Stages. The highest standards, especially at Key Stage 3, exist where it is recognised that pupils of all abilities need the active intervention of teachers to develop their individual skills. Pupils then show evidence of learning to read accurately and fluently and approach new reading, particularly of poetry, with confidence. A high standard of reading, particularly at Key Stage 4, has the additional qualities of responsiveness to imaginative or metaphorical language. Pupils read with considerable independence and discrimination and can undertake a wide range of texts for different purposes. When standards are low, pupils rarely read in a sustained way and individual support for pupils of average and above average ability is too infrequent. Skilled support for poor readers is a frequent problem; too often it is either not available or is too detached from the mainstream curriculum. Little attention is given by teachers or pupils to developing a programme of reading or recording progress.

Writing

12   Writing standards are somewhat lower at these key stages than those for other aspects of English. Standards are too low in a quarter of schools at Key Stage 3 and a fifth of schools at Key Stage 4. Strengths clearly outweigh weaknesses in about 40% of schools at both stages. Although standards are satisfactory for most pupils, concerns persist in these later key stages about consistency of quality across all aspects of writing. Pupils who write to high standards at Key Stage 3 show an ability to organise an extended text and to respond appropriately to the subject-matter as well as achieving accuracy in regular features of grammar, spelling and punctuation. In both key stages, but especially at Key Stage 4, pupils' writing increasingly shows a confident response to both literary and non-literary texts. At Key Stage 3 there is a good deal of experimenting with a variety of styles of writing. Low standards are revealed in a marked lack of variety, particularly at Key Stage 3, careless use of spelling and punctuation and a lack of any sense of

improvement through drafting. In some schools pupils do not acquire even minimal skills in information technology.

Post-16

13 Standards of achievement relative to pupils' capabilities are higher at post-16 than at other stages in all the main aspects of English, even allowing for differences in age and maturity. Pupils are highly motivated and the teaching is generally good. Standards are very good in 10% of lessons, and satisfactory or good in 80%. In 10% they are unsatisfactory or poor.

Quality of teaching

Key Stages 1 and 2

14 The quality of teaching at Key Stage 1 is satisfactory or better in 77% of lessons. It is good in 36%. The figures for Key Stage 2 are virtually identical. Across all schools, the most able pupils generally enjoy higher standards of teaching than those of average or lower ability, though this is not always apparent in mixed ability settings in any particular school.

15 At both key stages, good teaching is based on clear planning, a sound knowledge of National Curriculum requirements, the use of a range of effective teaching strategies and a clear understanding of the knowledge and skills that young children need. This is evident, for example, in reading where effective teachers show a command of teaching approaches and how to combine them as well as a wide knowledge of available children's literature. Positive motivation of pupils and the encouragement of orderly carrying out of tasks are also evident. At Key Stage 1 in particular good teaching involves frequent and sensitive interventions to help pupils to develop their spoken language in a variety of ways. Skilled use of adult help is also apparent. At Key Stage 2, good teaching provides a clear framework for pupils to learn collaboratively and with increasing autonomy. It also aims for maximum progress for individuals in reading and writing, based on effective monitoring and explicit teaching of reading and writing techniques.

16   Low-quality teaching is associated with poor lesson planning, a lack of differentiation between pupils when tasks are set, and too little direct teaching of skills. At Key Stage 1, the lack of challenge to individual pupils in the development of reading leads to underachievement by a minority of them. At Key Stage 2, over-reliance on published material and worksheets, unclear expectations and a lack of balance between whole class teaching and work with smaller groups are particular problems. In both key stages, but especially at Key Stage 2, inadequate knowledge about the English language and appropriate literature are serious handicaps for some teachers.

Key Stages 3 and 4

17   At Key Stage 3, the quality of teaching is satisfactory or better in 83% of lessons. It is good in 45% of lessons and unsatisfactory or poor in 17%. The equivalent figures for Key Stage 4 are 86%, 49% and 14%. Again, the most able pupils receive better teaching than those of average or lower ability.

18   An essential ingredient of high-quality teaching at these stages is the teacher's confident knowledge about language, understanding of the concept of literary genres, and acquaintance with a broad range of literary and non-fiction texts. The majority of teachers demonstrate these qualities but some do not: there are particular weaknesses in relation to familiarity with poetry and knowledge about language. There is also considerable uncertainty amongst teachers, particularly at Key Stage 3, about how to intervene positively to improve the individual reading abilities of all pupils. In some instances, the intellectual challenge of reading materials and tasks at Key Stage 3 is less than that of Key Stage 4, even allowing for age differences. Good teaching at these stages shows the basic qualities associated with Key Stages 1 and 2 but there are distinctive emphases on, for example, effective questioning to challenge and develop thought, the communication of aims to pupils, and explicit links which are understood by pupils between teaching and assessment procedures. Work related to the pupils' extra-curricular interests, for example in drama, is also conducive to good teaching. Low quality has characteristics similar to those found in the earlier stages though teachers' lack of specialist skills and knowledge are the most limiting. It is associated often with the practice of

differentiation by outcome rather than by matching tasks to the interests and abilities of pupils, so that the more able in particular are insufficiently stretched.

Post-16

19   The quality of post-16 teaching is satisfactory or better in 88% of lessons. It is better than satisfactory in 54% of lessons. There are indications that pupils of the lowest ability are taught less satisfactorily than others.

20   High-quality post-16 teaching is characterised by expert specialist knowledge and enthusiasm for the subject. Where lessons of low quality exist they arise most frequently from weak knowledge or poor methods such as the dictation of inflexible opinions.

Assessment, recording and reporting

21   At all levels, methods of assessment, recording and reporting which are shared between teachers and which are used to diagnose pupils' strengths and weaknesses and to inform planning are associated with high standards. Standards are satisfactory or better in about seven-eighths of schools in the secondary phase. In the primary phase the equivalent proportion is two-thirds.

22   At Key Stages 1 and 2, particular strengths are the regular assessment and diagnostic recording of pupils' reading ability, the good use of statutory tests and other tasks to inform planning, and the involvement of pupils in their own records of reading. Weaknesses are associated with the under-use of continuous assessment by the teacher, records which are not evaluative, and uninformative reporting to parents. At Key Stages 3 and 4 the most positive contributions to standards are associated with regular systematic contributions by pupils to the evaluation and recording of progress; and with formative use of assessment by teachers and pupils through, for example, review sheets attached to pupils' work. There are significant weaknesses arising from lack of co-ordination between school and departmental policies as well as between teachers. Also, too many teachers at Key Stage 3 fail

to diagnose accurately pupils' strengths and weaknesses in reading, in some cases because they are unsure how to do it.

Curriculum content

23   Attention to curriculum content is satisfactory or better in the majority of schools but there are weakness at all levels, with Key Stage 2 and middle schools giving greatest cause for concern.

24   At Key Stages 1 and 2, curriculum content is dealt with most satisfactorily when there is a policy in place which covers all the attainment targets and is closely related to detailed schemes and teaching approaches. In the majority of schools they are not sufficiently related, especially at Key Stage 2. Narrow or patchy coverage of programmes of study is a recurrent problem, leading to lack of balance in attention given to major aspects of English, such as the study of poetry. Lack of thorough planning to ensure effective coverage of all aspects of the programmes of study is the most frequent problem at Key Stage 3. Also at Key Stage 3 there are signs that increasing provision of time for reading has drawn attention to some teachers' lack of expertise in developing individual pupils' reading ability. Pupils with special educational needs are too cut off from the mainstream curriculum in a minority of the schools. At Key Stage 4 the GCSE syllabus is usually the main instrument of planning, with few more detailed schemes in evidence. As a result, the full range of study required by the National Curriculum is not always reflected in the pupils' work.

Provision for pupils with special educational needs

25   In the majority of schools in the sample, attention to pupils with special educational needs is satisfactory or better. In all four key stages it is most effective where careful provision is made for individual needs yet the SEN programme is not divorced from the mainstream curriculum.

26   Pupils with special educational needs are generally given effective support at Key Stage 1. There is good liaison between teachers and support staff; there are encouraging signs of effective support in reading and well-matched individual programmes help to raise standards.

These qualities are found less consistently at Key Stage 2 where the absence of special provision or appropriate differentiation in some cases causes underachievement and disadvantage. At Key Stage 3 there is a good response to individual needs and effective use of support staff is helping pupils to raise the standards of reading and writing. However, in a minority of schools, the excessive use of pupil withdrawal and a lack of co-ordination of SEN with mainstream programmes are persistent problems which tend, for example, to provide SEN pupils with an impoverished experience of literature.

Management and administration

27   In most schools, management and administration of English are satisfactory or better at all stages. However, there is a minority in which poor management is a factor in producing low standards.

28   At Key Stages 1 and 2, the role of the subject co-ordinator is highly significant. Where experienced co-ordinators plan clearly and work alongside other teachers to ensure effective implementation of a language policy, a benefit to pupils is evident. There are indications that in-service training programmes have been influential in this area. Inexperience and/or lack of time for the function seriously restrict the effectiveness of co-ordinators, factors particularly evident at Key Stage 2 in middle schools where lack of effective co-ordination adversely affects pupils' progress. At Key Stages 3 and 4, good departmental planning is an important factor in ensuring that all English teachers follow a coherent programme which exploits the National Curriculum effectively and links assessment of pupils to their progress. In a few schools there is no clear policy and little in the way of detailed or agreed plans. There are signs of a significant link between low standards and poor departmental management at Key Stages 3 and 4. When schools opt for early setting at Key Stage 3, boys too often predominate in lower English sets.

Resources and their management

29   The quality of teaching staff, teaching materials and accommodation is satisfactory or better in the majority of schools in this sample.

30   In this sample, virtually all teaching staff at all stages are appropriately qualified by their initial qualification or by subsequent training for the work they are doing. However, in-service needs are regularly identified especially in the areas of language co-ordination (Key Stages 1 and 2), techniques of teaching reading (Key Stages 2 and 3), teachers' formal knowledge about language (all stages), and, especially in secondary and middle schools, effective subject management.

31   There is consistent evidence that 10–15% of schools suffer from insufficient stocks of books, both quantitatively and in range. This is a particular handicap to able readers at Key Stages 2 and 3. Conversely, the presence of well-stocked libraries and professional librarians contributes to high standards.

Inspection issues

Inspection development

32   Inspections carried out under Section 9 of the Education (Schools) Act 1992 began in September 1993. Inspection teams have made a good start in meeting the requirements of the Framework for the Inspection of Schools. Inspectors of English are generally knowledgeable in the subject and the Framework. Early uncertainties have been resolved in many cases. This part of the subject profile draws together some of the key issues for further improving the quality and standard of inspection. Many issues are similar from one subject to another but where there are English-specific matters these are indicated.

33   Some examples of inspection writing are included. They are not intended to be viewed as models, but illustrate how some inspectors have met the Framework requirements. Most of the examples are extracts from longer texts.

Evidence gathering

34   Inspectors make full use of the time available to them and sample the range of work of different year groups, abilities and key stages across the compulsory years of education. Although the samples are often well balanced, inspectors should check that adequate attention is given to the range of age and ability in the school; also, to drama both in coverage and evaluation, and to pupils' knowledge about language. Where schools have sixth forms, post-16 work needs to be fairly represented in the sampling.

35   In reaching judgements, inspectors use evidence from a range of sources including lesson observation, departmental documents and discussions with pupils and teachers and samples of pupils' work. They need to ensure that these samples, especially of writing, are substantial enough to show in some depth the quality of work of individual or particular groups of pupils. Reading activities are frequently reported upon; reports are most effective where it is clear both what is being read and the quality of the pupils' response. The Supplementary Evidence Form provides a means of documenting evidence and

judgements from sources other than lessons and could be much more widely used. This is particularly important in relation to speaking and listening, where evidence from lessons alone can be quite limited.

Lesson Observation Forms

36   In general, Lesson Observation Forms are completed conscientiously. It is evident that inspectors are generally aware of the Framework criteria in making their observations. They need, though, to check that the full range of criteria relevant to the circumstances are used and that some subject detail and character show through.

37   In relation to the **content** of lessons, most inspectors adequately indicate the main activity. Further details of these activities, for example, what pupils are reading and what they are doing with it, would be helpful in setting the context. Inspectors should check that National Curriculum references are included where possible.

38   Responding to the Framework requirements to assess pupils' achievements in relation to national norms and taking account of pupils' abilities has not proved easy. In some lesson notes, there is little or no comment on standards under either heading. It is important that, wherever possible, judgements about the achievements of pupils are made. To support the judgements, inspectors should clearly identify what pupils know, understand and can do and set their achievements in the context of National Curriculum Statements of Attainment. Two examples are:

Year 3

Achievement (age referenced): Pupils were able to participate actively in discussions and were tolerant of views of others. Achievement in writing, spelling and handwriting was appropriate for pupils' ages. Achievement in speaking and listening ranged levels 2–3, writing and spelling level 2, handwriting level 2. Grade 3

Year 10

Achievement (taking account of pupils' abilities): Excellent. Discussion of high quality from a group of students who understood well how to collaborate and utilise the idea of the whole group. Very impressive levels of attainment here. High order skills of analysis, synthesis, discrimination. Pupils, described by the school as the "special needs" English group, were performing well above what might have been expected. Grade 1

39   Inspectors usually cite relevant evidence when judging the quality of teaching, and evaluation is based on the criteria in the Framework though there is a tendency to concentrate on planning and provision. There is a need to ensure that all aspects of the criteria and the impact on achievement and learning are evaluated.

Year 10

Clear and confident handling of class – good rapport. Well planned – written tasks allowed for range of abilities and personal response. Differentiated worksheet prepared for pupils. Time limits accurately set – purposeful pace. Work carefully and constructively marked for redrafting. Homework carefully set. Grade 2.

Year 3/4

Timing of activity was not appropriate to time of day. Some of class restless. No differentiation in word lists – task did not match needs of all pupils. Story – appropriate for range of ability and as link with project on canals. Insufficient time for satisfactory length of story reading – time left after spellings did not allow good introduction to book. Grade 4.

40   Inspectors could make more use of the Lesson Observation Form to record the impact of contributory factors on standards and the quality of teaching and learning.

Subject Evidence Forms

41   Subject Evidence Forms are usually fully completed and in most cases it is evident that judgements are based on a good range of evidence. Inspectors need to check that this is sufficiently explicit about pupils' standards of achievement in and the quality of learning and teaching of all aspects of English.

42   Extracts relating to standards of achievement and to the quality of learning and teaching from Subject Evidence Forms follow.

Standards of Achievement

KS 3 & 4: ...There are no significant differences in the pattern of achievement between the 2 Key Stages. There is, however, a marked difference in the standards achieved and progress made by pupils of lower and of upper ability. Lower ability pupils of all ages have made clear progress and are achieving unusually high standards in ATs 2 and 3 especially. Upper ability pupils, of whom there is a relatively small proportion in the school, demonstrate a degree of underachievement linked to their low motivation. Writing of the highest quality was not encountered at all, though there was acceptable all-round competence in the 3 ATs. ...

Quality of Learning

KS1 & 2: . . . Young children are encouraged to use a range of strategies for reading, including phonic skills, picture and context cues and word recognition. Some less successful older readers use too narrow a range of strategies to help them read. Pupils enjoy selecting books. Some need guidance in selecting from a wider range. Older pupils write book reviews and are developing critical discernment. They understand how to use an index and other organisational features but their independent research skills are less well developed. ...

Quality of Teaching

KS4: . . . At KS4, the quality of the teaching seen was good. Teachers were well skilled in handling and motivating pupils, and set consistent guidelines for work and behaviour. Teachers had positive relationships with pupils and supported pupil:pupil relationships sensitively. Lessons were well planned, with clear targets set for pupils, and time was managed successfully to maintain interest and involvement. Good use was made of the limited range of resources and sequences of work were carefully constructed to involve all pupils. The least able pupils were supported sensitively and there was evidence of careful preparation of resources for those pupils, as well as for pupils with English as a second language. There was, however, less evidence of challenge or extended work for higher attaining pupils and, in general, work was pitched to the lower end of the ability range. ...

43   Inspectors clearly assemble much evidence and make judgements about the resource provision for English and features such as the organisation, management and procedures in the subject including assessment arrangements. The impact of these on pupils' achievements and the quality of learning is the central issue which should feature prominently in the evaluation.

Judgement Recording Statements

44   The proformas of Judgement Recording Statements are usually fully completed. It is important that the recorded judgements take full account of all available evidence. The purpose and use of Judgement Recording Statements are outlined in Appendix C of Part 3 of the *Handbook for the Inspection of Schools*.

Subject sections in inspection reports

45   Subject sections in reports are usually carefully written and are consistent with the evidence contained in the Subject Evidence Form. Inspectors need to check that appropriate weight is given to comments about standards of achievement and the quality of learning in relation to teaching and the range of other features, and that the distinctive characteristics of the subject feature in the writing. Judgements should be clear and succinct and draw on all the evidence available. The extracts from subject reports which follow focus on standards of achievement in English.

School A

.... Standards of achievement in English are above average and are satisfactory or better in relation to pupils' capabilities. Pupils enter school with a well-developed awareness of print and a familiarity with books. They are well supported by the school and generally read and write at an early age, using phonic skills, picture and content cues and word recognition. The school encourages parents to share in their children's reading. Pupils in both key stages read with fluency and accuracy. Their ability to infer meaning and to use research skills to find information is less well developed. Some could be encouraged to read more widely beyond the reading scheme. ....

School B

....Oral work is a notable strength of the department. Pupils are generally open and sensitive towards each other. In small groups they help one another express ideas or opinions; they are able to keep on task for long periods and to work independently of the teachers. Thorough records are kept of the pupils' oral work. The good work done in drama lessons and clubs and some pupils' involvement in various public speaking competitions encourage high standards of speaking and listening. ....

School C

....The overall quality of writing throughout the school is unsatisfactory. Although some pupils do write creatively, including the writing of their own plays and poems, there is little writing for a range of audiences and some of the work is of limited value. There are insufficient opportunities for drafting and using information technology and pupils' skills in these areas are under-developed. Standards of spelling are not high. Spelling is not taught on a regular basis and has not been included in the language policy as a separate element. Skill in the use of dictionaries is undeveloped.

46   In writing to the Framework requirements, inspectors need to ensure that a judgement is made about the school's compliance with statutory requirements and that any action which is needed, if any, to develop the subject is clearly expressed. This is helpful to schools in their action planning.

The interpretation of subject performance data

National Curriculum assessment

47   At Key Stage 1, almost 80% of pupils were assessed by their teachers as achieving level 2 or above in English. Teacher assessments (TA) and test scores for the four aspects of English tested were:

	TA	TEST
Reading	80%	80%
Writing	70%	67%
Spelling	73%	71%
Handwriting	81%	80%

Girls out-performed boys in all the four aspects tested.

48   At Key Stage 3, the published national results are based on the responses from a small minority of maintained schools. They need, therefore, to be treated with caution. These show that the percentages of pupils achieving level 5 or above were 63% (teacher assessment) and 58% (test). Girls considerably out-performed boys in both teacher assessment and the test.

GCSE

49   The large majority of 15-year-olds, more than 80%, take GCSE English. The average points score for all pupils in maintained schools in 1994 was 4.59 but this figure disguises a substantial difference in performance between girls (4.91) and boys (4.26). Inspectors should note such differences in individual schools, enquire into their causes and assess the steps being taken to overcome them.

50   A smaller but still substantial number of pupils enter for GCSE English literature. More girls than boys take the examination and they perform better than boys; their average points score in 1994 was 4.97 compared with 4.42 for boys. The average for all pupils was 4.66. It is important that inspectors consider the school's entry policy for literature and its effects on the quality and extent of all pupils' reading.

51 When relevant, inspectors should also comment on GCSE results in drama and in communication studies. In both these subjects, girls out-perform boys. In drama, the average points score in 1994 was 5.09 (girls 5.31; boys 4.73). In communication studies it was 4.41 (girls 4.75; boys 3.99). A particular point to comment on in relation to communication studies is the ability range of the pupils entered for it.

In making comparative judgements, inspectors should note that:

- year-on-year comparisons may be affected by substantial changes in assessment requirements, particularly the shifting balance between coursework and examinations;

- comparisons with other core subjects should be based mainly on the average points score for English.

GCE A/AS

52 The numbers of pupils entered for A-level English subjects have increased steadily in recent years.

53 English literature is the most popular choice but English language and communication studies are well-established minority subjects. In all of them, entries from girls outnumber those from boys by approximately 2:1. Girls also out-perform boys in all three subjects though the differences are less marked than in GCSE. In drama, where the overall entry is very small, the gender difference in entries is even more marked but in 1994 the performance of boys was slightly higher than that of girls.

54 The percentages of pupils gaining A–E grades in 1994 were 90.4 in English literature, 86.6 in English language, 83.0 in communication studies and 94.4 in drama. Overall, the data for drama suggest that the subject is taken by a small, talented and highly-motivated group of students; a hypothesis which inspectors might wish to test. Inspectors need to approach year-on-year comparisons with caution in English subjects because of the increased emphasis on examinations in their assessment.

55 GCE AS entries in these subjects are low nationally and any comparisons need to be made with caution.

Annex A

GCSE results for 15 year olds¹ for English 1994

Type of School		Number of 15 year old pupils entered	Percentages achieving grades									1994			1993		1992²	
			A*	A	B	C	D	E	F	G	U	Average points score³	% A*-C grades	% A*-G grades	Average points score³	% A-C grades	Average points score³	% A-C grades
Comprehensive		409591	1.3	6.9	17.9	26.7	20.9	12.0	8.8	2.1	0.3	4.54	52.8	96.7	4.40	51.5	4.39	50.1
Selective		16429	5.4	28.5	42.9	18.9	2.9	0.6	0.4	0.1	0.0	6.11	95.8	99.7	6.07	97.3	5.92	93.5
Modern		15160	0.3	2.9	12.7	27.3	23.9	15.5	11.5	2.2	0.4	4.18	43.2	96.3	4.02	38.6	3.92	34.8
Maintained	All pupils	441180	1.4	7.6	18.7	26.4	20.3	11.7	8.6	2.1	0.3	4.59	54.1	96.8	4.45	53.0	4.41	50.7
	Boys	220588	0.9	5.2	14.6	24.2	21.9	14.4	11.8	3.1	0.5	4.26	45.0	96.2	4.14	44.2	4.09	41.7
	Girls	220592	1.9	10.0	22.7	28.6	18.8	9.0	5.4	1.0	0.1	4.91	63.2	97.3	4.77	61.7	4.73	59.4
All Subjects Maintained	All pupils		2.1	8.4	16.4	20.5	18.9	14.5	10.2	4.5	1.5	4.40	47.4	95.5	4.12	46.3	4.14	45.0

1 Aged 15 on 31/8/93

2 1992 results include a small amount of data from special schools

3 Calculated on basis A*=8, A=7, B=6, C=5, D=4, E=3, F=2, G=1

– less than 100 candidates

* more than 100 and less than 500 candidates

GCSE results for 15 year olds[1] for English Literature 1994

Type of School		Number of 15 year old pupils entered	Percentages achieving grades									1994 Average points score[3]	% A*–C grades	% A*–G grades	1993 Average points score[3]	% A–C grades	1992[2] Average points score[3]	% A–C grades
			A*	A	B	C	D	E	F	G	U							
Comprehensive		332399	1.7	8.4	19.8	26.8	18.3	11.9	8.0	2.2	0.5	4.66	56.7	97.0	4.55	55.3	4.54	53.7
Selective		16006	5.2	25.1	38.8	23.2	5.3	1.3	0.5	0.1	0.0	5.95	92.3	99.6	5.97	75.5	5.93	94.5
Modern		10070	0.3	3.8	14.8	28.8	21.8	15.2	9.5	2.7	0.3	4.30	47.7	97.0	4.13	42.5	4.11	39.7
Maintained	All pupils	358475	1.8	9.0	20.6	26.7	17.8	11.5	7.7	2.1	0.4	4.71	58.1	97.1	4.59	56.5	4.57	54.5
	Boys	169987	1.2	6.6	17.0	25.2	19.1	13.8	10.4	3.1	0.7	4.42	50.0	96.4	4.30	48.6	4.27	46.2
	Girls	188488	2.3	11.2	23.8	28.0	16.7	9.4	5.3	1.1	0.2	4.97	65.3	97.7	4.86	63.8	4.82	61.7
All Subjects Maintained	All pupils		2.1	8.4	16.4	20.5	18.9	14.5	10.2	4.5	1.5	4.40	47.4	95.5	4.12	46.3	4.14	45.0

1 Aged 15 on 31/8/93
2 1992 results include a small amount of data from special schools
3 Calculated on basis A*=8, A=7, B=6, C=5, D=4, E=3, F=2, G=1

– less than 100 candidates
* more than 100 and less than 500 candidates
x information not available

GCSE results for 15 year olds[1] for Communication Studies 1994

Type of School		Number of 15 year old pupils entered	Percentages achieving grades									Average points score[3]	% A*-C grades	% A*-G grades	Average points score[3]	% A-C grades	Average points score[3]	% A-C grades
			A*	A	B	C	D	E	F	G	U	1994			1993		1992[2]	
Comprehensive		26439	2.1	8.0	15.4	20.3	19.5	15.5	9.7	3.8	0.8	4.40	45.9	94.3	4.03	43.7	3.64	34.5
Selective		374	4.3	24.6	35.0	26.7	7.5	1.1	0.0	0.0	0.0	5.88	90.6	99.2	5.73	85.8	–	–
Modern		762	1.3	3.5	11.0	18.2	22.8	20.9	12.2	5.1	1.4	3.95	34.1	95.1	3.97	39.0	–	–
Maintained	All pupils	27575	2.1	8.1	15.6	20.4	19.5	15.4	9.6	3.8	0.8	4.41	46.2	94.4	4.06	44.1	3.66	34.5
	Boys	12610	0.8	5.3	12.0	17.7	19.7	18.2	13.3	5.6	1.3	3.99	35.8	92.7	3.66	34.3	–	–
	Girls	14965	3.1	10.5	18.6	22.6	19.2	13.1	6.5	2.2	0.5	4.75	54.9	95.9	4.40	52.6	–	–
All Subjects Maintained	All pupils		2.1	8.4	16.4	20.5	18.9	14.5	10.2	4.5	1.5	4.40	47.4	95.5	4.12	46.3	4.14	45.0

1 Aged 15 on 31/8/93
2 1992 results include a small amount of data from special schools
3 Calculated on basis A*=8, A=7, B=6, C=5, D=4, E=3, F=2, G=1

– less than 100 candidates
* more than 100 and less than 500 candidates
x information not available

GCSE results for 15 year olds[1] for Drama 1994

Type of School		Number of 15[1] year old pupils entered	Percentages achieving grades									Average points score[3]	% A*–C grades	% A*–G grades	Average points score[3]	% A–C grades	Average points score[3]	% A–C grades
			1994												**1993**		**1992[2]**	
			A*	A	B	C	D	E	F	G	U							
Comprehensive		55641	2.2	14.6	24.4	25.1	15.1	8.9	4.3	1.7	0.5	5.08	66.3	96.2	4.79	63.6	4.93	64.4
Selective		1114	5.6	32.2	39.2	16.3	4.3	0.7	0.6	0.2	0.0	6.13	93.4	99.2	5.95	93.2	5.93	92.9
Modern		1738	0.7	9.7	21.8	26.1	20.7	11.5	4.7	1.3	0.5	4.80	58.3	96.5	4.60	59.4	4.69	59.4
Maintained	All pupils	58493	2.2	14.8	24.6	24.9	15.1	8.8	4.3	1.6	0.5	5.09	66.5	96.3	4.80	64.0	4.93	64.6
	Boys	22377	1.3	10.3	20.4	24.9	17.6	11.6	6.4	2.6	0.9	4.73	56.9	95.1	4.38	53.9	4.55	54.5
	Girls	36116	2.8	17.6	27.1	24.9	13.5	7.0	2.9	1.0	0.3	5.31	72.5	97.0	5.06	70.1	5.15	70.3
All Subjects Maintained	All pupils		2.1	8.4	16.4	20.5	18.9	14.5	10.2	4.5	1.5	4.40	47.4	95.5	4.12	46.3	4.14	45.0

1 Aged 15 on 31/8/93
2 1992 results include a small amount of data from special schools
3 Calculated on basis A*=8, A=7, B=6, C=5, D=4, E=3, F=2, G=1

– less than 100 candidates
* more than 100 and less than 500 candidates
x information not available

Annex B

GCE AS results for English Language 1994

Type of School		Number of candidates	1994							% A–B grades	% A–E grades	Average points score[p]	1993 % A–B grades	1993 % A–E grades	1992 % A–B grades	1992 % A–E grades
			Percentages achieving grades													
			A	B	C	D	E	N	U							
Maintained	All pupils	799	6.6	14.1	21.7	26.9	18.4	6.6	4.5	20.8	87.7	2.3	21.0	86.4	20.9	83.4
	Boys	350	6.3	13.7	18.6	23.7	23.1	7.4	5.7	20.0	85.4	2.1	20.2	87.4	18.4	83.5
	Girls	449	6.9	14.5	24.1	29.4	14.7	6.0	3.6	21.4	89.5	2.4	21.6	85.6	22.8	83.3
All subjects Maintained	All pupils		7.1	10.2	14.8	17.9	18.2	12.9	15.1	17.3	68.2	1.8	17.0	65.5	16.6	65.4

– less than 100 candidates

* more than 100 and less than 500 candidates

p Calculated on basis A=5, B=4, C=3, D=2, E=1

The number of pupils taking AS levels is insufficient to yield a meaningful analysis by type of maintained school

GCE AS results for English Literature* 1994

Type of School		Number of candidates	Percentages achieving grades							% A–B grades	% A–E grades	Average points score[p]	1993 % A–B grades	1993 % A–E grades	1992 % A–B grades	1992 % A–E grades
			A	B	C	D	E	N	U							
Maintained	All pupils	349	5.2	9.5	15.8	29.8	22.6	11.7	2.9	14.6	82.8	1.9	10.0	78.2	15.2	83.6
	Boys	137	5.8	11.7	15.3	28.5	20.4	11.7	1.5	17.5	81.8	2.0	10.1	79.0	13.2	81.2
	Girls	212	4.7	8.0	16.0	30.7	24.1	11.8	3.8	12.7	83.5	1.9	9.9	77.8	16.2	84.9
All subjects																
Maintained	All pupils		7.1	10.2	14.8	17.9	18.2	12.9	15.1	17.3	68.2	1.8	17.0	65.5	16.6	65.4

– less than 100 candidates

* more than 100 and less than 500 candidates

p Calculated on basis A=5, B=4, C=3, D=2, E=1

The number of pupils taking AS levels is insufficient to yield a meaningful analysis by type of maintained school

GCE AS results for Communication Studies* 1994

Type of School		Number of candidates	Percentages achieving grades							% A–B grades	% A–E grades	Average points score[p]	1993 % A–B grades	% A–E grades	1992 % A–B grades	% A–E grades
			A	B	C	D	E	N	U							
Maintained	All pupils	259	9.3	18.5	18.9	18.9	10.4	4.6	0.8	27.8	76.1	2.3	–	–	–	–
	Boys	70	–	–	–	–	–	–	–	–	–	–	–	–	–	–
	Girls	189	10.1	21.2	20.6	18.5	8.5	4.8	0.5	31.2	78.8	2.4	–	–	–	–
All subjects Maintained	All pupils		7.1	10.2	14.8	17.9	18.2	12.9	15.1	17.3	68.2	1.8	17.0	65.5	16.6	65.4

– less than 100 candidates

* more than 100 and less than 500 candidates

p Calculated on basis A=5, B=4, C=3, D=2, E=1

The number of pupils taking AS levels is insufficient to yield a meaningful analysis by type of maintained school

GCE A-Level results for English Language 1994

Type of School		Number of candidates	1994							% A-B grades	% A-E grades	1993 % A-B grades	% A-E grades	1992 % A-B grades	% A-E grades
			A	B	C	D	E	N	U						
Comprehensive		4906	9.9	18.3	20.3	21.6	15.9	8.4	4.9	28.3	86.0	26.4	82.7	16.8	86.5
Selective		505	13.7	28.1	24.0	17.4	12.1	2.8	1.6	41.8	95.2	41.3	88.4	25.9	90.9
Modern		84	−	−	−	−	−	−	−	−	−	10.4	72.6	15.3	82.1
Maintained	All pupils	5495	10.1	19.0	20.6	21.3	15.6	8.1	4.6	29.2	86.6	27.2	82.9	17.4	86.7
	Boys	1889	10.1	18.3	20.0	21.2	15.7	8.8	5.5	28.3	85.2	24.9	81.6	17.0	85.8
	Girls	3606	10.2	19.4	20.9	21.4	15.5	7.7	4.2	29.6	87.4	28.3	83.6	17.6	87.1
All subjects Maintained	All pupils		13.1	16.2	18.5	18.9	15.2	9.4	7.5	29.3	81.9	28.0	79.7	26.4	78.6

− less than 100 candidates

* more than 100 and less than 500 candidates

GCE A-Level results for English Literature 1994

Type of School		Number of candidates	1994 Percentages achieving grades							1994 % A–B grades	1994 % A–E grades	1993 % A–B grades	1993 % A–E grades	1992 % A–B grades	1992 % A–E grades
			A	B	C	D	E	N	U						
Comprehensive		24944	12.1	16.9	21.6	22.6	16.4	6.8	2.8	29.0	89.6	27.2	87.6	29.1	86.7
Selective		4070	22.3	25.4	22.9	17.7	8.2	2.8	0.6	47.6	96.4	41.0	94.2	43.1	92.7
Modern		346	7.2	8.7	18.8	25.1	19.9	10.4	8.4	15.9	79.8	15.2	69.9	19.8	83.2
Maintained	All pupils	29360	13.5	18.0	21.7	22.0	15.3	6.3	2.6	31.4	90.4	29.0	88.3	30.5	87.3
	Boys	8854	13.9	16.9	20.7	21.7	15.7	6.8	3.3	30.7	88.8	29.3	86.8	30.0	85.7
	Girls	20506	13.3	18.4	22.2	22.1	15.1	6.0	2.2	31.7	91.1	28.9	89.0	30.6	87.9
All subjects Maintained	All pupils		13.1	16.2	18.5	18.9	15.2	9.4	7.5	29.3	81.9	28.0	79.7	26.4	78.6

– less than 100 candidates

* more than 100 and less than 500 candidates

GCE A-Level results for Communication Studies 1994

Type of School		Number of candidates	1994									1993		1992	
			Percentages achieving grades							% A–B grades	% A–E grades	% A–B grades	% A–E grades	% A–B grades	% A–E grades
			A	B	C	D	E	N	U						
Comprehensive		4980	10.5	14.9	18.9	21.7	16.4	10.1	6.1	25.3	82.4	25.5	84.1	21.1	82.5
Selective		449	18.7	15.6	25.6	19.2	10.5	6.9	2.4	34.3	89.5	36.4	89.2	30.1	92.9
Modern		126	3.2	13.5	23.0	28.6	16.7	6.3	6.3	16.7	84.9	17.0	82.1	19.3	82.1
Maintained	All pupils	5555	11.0	14.9	19.6	21.7	15.9	9.8	5.9	25.9	83.0	26.1	84.5	21.5	83.2
	Boys	1866	8.2	12.6	19.9	22.2	15.8	11.8	7.8	20.8	78.6	22.4	79.6	18.5	79.4
	Girls	3689	12.4	16.0	19.4	21.4	16.0	8.8	4.9	28.4	85.2	27.9	86.8	22.8	84.7
All subjects Maintained	All pupils		13.1	16.2	18.5	18.9	15.2	9.4	7.5	29.3	81.9	28.0	79.7	26.4	78.6

— less than 100 candidates

* more than 100 and less than 500 candidates

GCE A-Level results for Drama 1994

Type of School		Number of candidates	Percentages achieving grades							1994 % A–B grades	1994 % A–E grades	1993 % A–B grades	1993 % A–E grades	1992 % A–B grades	1992 % A–E grades
			A	B	C	D	E	N	U						
Comprehensive		562	19.2	26.0	28.3	16.0	5.3	0.4	0.4	45.2	94.8	44.4	97.8	–	–
Selective		8	–	–	–	–	–	–	–	–	–	–	–	–	–
Modern		6	–	–	–	–	–	–	–	–	–	–	–	–	–
Maintained	All pupils	576	19.1	25.5	28.5	15.8	5.6	0.3	0.3	44.6	94.4	43.1	96.7	–	–
	Boys	130	24.6	19.2	29.2	16.2	4.6	0.8	0.8	43.8	93.8	44.2	95.8	–	–
	Girls	446	17.5	27.4	28.3	15.7	5.8	0.2	0.2	44.8	94.6	42.6	97.0	–	–
All subjects Maintained	All pupils		13.1	16.2	18.5	18.9	15.2	9.4	7.5	29.3	81.9	28.0	79.7	26.4	78.6

– less than 100 candidates
* more than 100 and less than 500 candidates

Printed in the United Kingdom for HMSO
Dd300291 4/95 C130 G3397 10170